# THE EINTOU

Kf.w M Kht

Ysw inform: It is not our task to make horses drink water; neither is it to lead them to water; it is not even to tell them where water is; rather our task is to let horses know water exists. When their thirst gets strong enough, they will, of their own devices, seek it and drink what they need to live. Should they never endeavor towards the water, it means they prefer death to life. It is not our task to tell horses whether they should prefer life or death. It is to allow them to live or die as they prefer.

## Table of Contents

iii

iv

## DEDICATION

To Jabari & Kiri'Anna, my Eintous.

∞

To Gwnstr & Nstr: I endeavor always to make you proud I am one of you.

To Nicole Shannon who returned me to her heart as "Pops," and who answers my phone calls even though I call from an "android."

And to mothers everywhere whose children have been murdered in the name of religion, race, oppression, and other injustices.

# DIBAJI

January 25th, 2000. One week earlier, Mwt[1] of my mswt[2] had given birth to our second child- a daughter. We sat in the living room of our home- Mwt on the couch breastfeeding and fawning over the ⊔[3] She had fashioned for nine months; and I sat across from them play wrestling with our 1 ½ year old son- "Tickle and Tackle Monster" as I affectionately called it. I paused a moment to consider Mwt and my daughter as my son, laughing his little head off, tried to wrestle me to the floor.

They looked like Sr.t and Hr.w[4], the way the sunlight captured and surrounded them. The beauty of it caught me by surprise. I was awe stricken. "This is my family," I thought to myself, "Mwt, my mswt, my home."

---

[1] Mwt- "The Mother." It is still a great source of sadness that during our divorce, Mwt did not understand and considered it insult that I referred to her as "The Mother." It pains me to this day white ignorance who surrounded her convinced her I was trying to insult her.
[2] Children
[3] Kh (Ka), life force, or soul.
[4] Popularly and incorrectly "Isis" and "Horus."

I took my still giggling son into my arms, carried him and sat next to Mwt and my daughter. I kissed Her gently on the forehead. I thanked Her for blessing our family with two beautiful mswt; I thanked Her for keeping us alive. I ran my right thumb along my daughter's forehead, etching Gwnhk.[5] I did the same to my son, who at that point, sat still in my lap vigorously sucking on his "adas" (how he pronounced "pacifier"). Our mswt represent new cycles in the histories of our families; they represent continuations of our lines- male and female- that began during p't nnw p't.[6] They bridge fulfillment of our past with infinite potential, that is the hopes within our future.

Mwt, having finished breast feeding, handed Kiri'Anna to me. It was time for them both to rest, and from the moment she arrived on this planet, I was the only person who could get her to sleep.

---

[5] Gwnhk symbolizes cyclic, energetic infinity and the connections binding us to Tp'wy (our ancestors).
[6] Beginnings of beginnings

I gently nudged Jabari to my side as I positioned his sister over my heart and began softly humming a lullaby while gently patting her back. She snuggled as her breathing slowly synchronized with my heartbeats. She seemed to lovingly watch her brother as they drifted into baby dream worlds.

They were my poetry, the two of them- the words and the form it took. They inspired me in ways and on levels I- to this day- cannot adequately describe. They brought to the surface emotions that lay dormant deep within me. In many instances, staring at the two of them, I uncovered emotions I did not think I, as a man, had (or could have). These emotions swelled until they reached boiling points. They more often than not erupted into poems; poems I created for them to read one day; to consider when they became adults; poems that would let them know, whatever became of them, whatever their lives would eventually become, there were moments like these during which they filled me with such love, warmth, and wonder. I needed to let them know (and hopefully they would remember) there were times when they encompassed my entire world

3

and there was nothing ever imagined or created more important to me than them.

I wanted to leave them something concrete; something that, whenever encountered, they would know represented them, our lives together, and the enormous and endless love I have for them.

Moreover, I wanted it to encompass all that we are as descendants of those who precede us; Our traditions, our melodies and rhythms as a people; I wanted it to connect us to The Nchi Ya Mababu (Land of the Ancestors- that is, "Africa") and to the magnificence She offers the world; I wanted it to connect us to everything that has ever emanated from Her; I wanted it to connect us to all Her mswt and their stories on this planet.

And so that day- 25 January 2000, one week after Kiri'Anna's birth- I began researching us. I dove into the histories of my immediate and extended families; I began conversing with Mwt's father, who regaled stories infused with Haitian history. He told me how, when his ancestors triumphed over Napolean and secured their freedom, one of their first orders of business was assisting with the

4

emancipation of Georgia's (American South) enslaved; he told me of the significance of the conch shell to Haitian history and culture.

I researched Haitian, African American, and African, religious practices, and cultural philosophies. I saw continuity- how everything circles back upon itself; how our cultures, our music, our very selves represent arcs within Nchi Ya Mababu's continuity.[7]

As I researched our music, I noticed no matter where or how we composed, there was embedded within it layers. Layers that were sometimes coherent and fluid and at other times ran counter to or against main beats. I began to grasp the significance of Jazz syncopations, for example, and how that language evolved from ancestral practices of communicating in haphazard, (seemingly) nonsensical, broken and antigrammatic while voices simultaneously communicating

---

[7] I even attempted to develop a family culture, philosophy, and symbolisms that combined African American and Haitian cultures for the children, but I abandoned the attempt because Mwt and her family, rooted in christianity and not fully grasping the concept, belittled my efforts.

TheNegroSpirituals and important survival information took new on fascinatingly studied as I meaninged- how those ingenious people oftenrightinfrontof their) oppressors' escaped meetings, coordinated, and planned (faces!

I came to see profound and sustained resistance to racism, religionism, injustice, and oppression within the (sometimes) seemingly defeatist, melismatic, and self-denigrating eruptions of "Field Hollers," which had their foundations in African linguistic practices, evolved into the Blues, and finally found their way into modern Rap and Hip-Hop lyrics.

I came to grasp and appreciate rather than succumbing to oppression and injustice, in the face of overwhelming odds, our ancestors resisted. They never caved- even when, to observers- they seemed to give up. They embedded their resistance within their languages, religious practices, music- and even dance!

This led me to reconsider my own family's communication practices- how elders would often, when instructing or guiding us, render their wisdoms in short, powerful "sayings." I recalled sometimes hearing my grandfather say, "here's a pearl for you," and then offer compact wisdom. Or he would say "you missed your pearl" when someone didn't heed the wisdom of an elder. (It also occurred to me back then "pearls" could represent the "offspring" of oysters and other bivalve mollusks.)[8]

And so, the form I wanted to create for my mswt began to take shape. I knew it had to encompass our syncopated rhythms; I knew it had to employ highly metaphorical, connotative, and heightened language, whose rhythms varied from coherence to running counter to its primary beats; I knew the form had to tie my children to the whole of Nchi Ya Mababu's story and Her diasporic peoples; I knew the form had to carry short, powerful messages of resistance to and triumphs over impossible odds, injustice, and oppression; moreover, I knew the form had to carry what I understood to be overarching Nchi Ya Mababu philosophy- that is, we return- we always

---

[8] I later learned pearls are not actual "offspring" so much as they are by-products of defense mechanisms.

return to that from which we come. And so, my initial name for the burgeoning form-"Pearls."

But what would these Pearls look like on paper? How could the form reflect the name? How could I create a form that had structure and rules but simultaneously allowed for freedoms of improvisation which violated those "rules" while not violating the form itself? (What I would later identify as its "bluesy/jazzy" nature.)

I began researching short, powerful poetic forms (American Cinquains, Haikus, and Tankas primarily). I was particularly struck by Haiku "kireji" or cutting word, which to me seemed to embed quick and powerful shifts within its rhythms. To me kireji seemed to represent sharp turns that went against the set rhythm and flow of the poem, and that (perceived) syncopation appealed to me; however, my Pearls could not be restricted to any one subject or theme (e.g. nature) as they had to encompass or express the expanse of experiences throughout Ourstory. The last line of the American Cinquain struck me as "kireji-like" in its sudden and abrupt break from the poem's established flow and rhythm. To me these breaks lend greater power to the forms' impact. And if nothing else, I wanted Pearls to be powerful.

Not only powerful, but I also wanted them to be compact and easily recited; something that when written well, stayed with readers' memory long after they put the poem down. But how long would be long enough without being too long? It could not be three or five lines long because I felt that would be too mimicry- coming off as Haiku or American cinquain knock offs (and Black poetry was already seen- in some circles- as european mimics). I wrestled with the matter of length for days. And then- by chance- I found my answer within Nchi Ya Mababu's deep story, within the symbolism of Her greatest civilization, Km.t!

In Kmtyw psychospiritualism, the number seven represents completion or resurrection, which to me fit ideally within the concept of the Pearl in as much as its cyclic nature would symbolize 360*- the serpent eating its tail, in a sense. Also, in the psychospiritual symbolisms of the Dogon of Western Nchi Ya Mababu, the number three represents male energy and four represents female energy; the two combined represent perfection; further when a man and woman unite, they find completion of their union (and resurrection of themselves) within mswt. This idea- 3+4= the Pearl- placed a nice bow on the form's presentation and significance both within my family and Nchi Ya Mababu's diasporan cultures. It did not take me long to settle on seven lines as the Pearl's form. But seven lines of what?

I had settled on the form being syllabic (but not necessarily iambic) or word count in nature. After experimenting with different syllable lengths, I settled on even numbered syllables per line because it seemed easier to incorporate blues rhythms into the form; I settled on the syllabic (or word) count 2-4-6-8-6-4-2. I had accomplished everything I set out to achieve with the form- or so I thought.

During the first week of February 2000, I sat in my office as Jabari played on a pallet his mother had prepared for him and his sister's little arms and legs were bundled within the BJÖRN her mother strapped to me. I was thumbing through Doctor Molefi Asante's book "The African Names" for no other reason than wasting time when I came across the Western Nchi Ya Mababu word (or name) "Eintou," translated as pearl. There was something in the way it was spelled and the way I pronounced it- AH-n-TOO- that appealed to me. I repeated it for measure, and Jabari, almost seeming to approve, repeated after me. I cannot be sure, but I am quite positive Kiri'Anna lifted her little head and smiled at me as though she also approved. That sealed it! everything fell into place. She was my poetry, and He was the form it took. From that moment on they were my Eintous.

I sat in that moment of accomplishment as Jabari's powerfully brown eyes seemed to lock on mine. I grabbed a note pad from my desk, thought a moment and then:

> **HIS EYES**
>
> I stare
> Into his eyes
> And hope he sees all that
> He used to be staring through me
> And when my son's eyes blink
> What I will be
> Stares back

The first Eintou ever written, inspired by the bravely quiet and powerful eyes of my infant warrior.

It seemed as though I offered the right word to the 𓏏𓀀𓅓𓇌𓏤 [9] because Wpwt [10] immediately began opening other ways for me to connect the Eintou to Ourstory. Over the next several months, as I experimented with and became comfortable writing the form, it revealed more of its hidden connections.

I observed when I wrote Eintous centered on the page, they appeared to be little MrKB,[11]

---

[9] Ymyw.h't or ancestors. Tranlated those who are in front.

[10] Opener of Ways: in Kmtyw psychospiritualism, this represented the principle by which we ascend to higher consciousness.

and the fourth line (consisting of eight syllables or words) seemed to be the point around which Eintous revolved. The Eintou seemed to ascend toward that fourth line and continue upward as it ended. This immediately suggested Kmtyw beliefs that deceased (and even living) souls journey through the Dwt[12] seeking to emerge on the Eastern Horizon as ascended (solar) Ntr Consciousness. The fourth line, or Kht (horizon) as I would name it, symbolized how a reader's consciousness flowed through an Eintou as it was read. That is to say, readers navigate its first three lines entering comprehension of its message (they enter the Dwt); then, and as they approach the Kht, they grasp surface understanding; Once they cross the Kht and ascend to the last three lines, understanding of the Eintou's deeper meanings and messages (crossing the horizon into higher consciousness) dawns on them.

An important aspect of the Eintou as it relates to Kmtyw psychospiritualism is the Ysw[13]

---

[11] "Pyramids."
[12] Underworld souls navigated to reach higher consciousness.
[13] Ancient Ones

viewed their world from North to South; that is Southern Km.t was "upper," and Northern Km.t "lower." The Eintou is read from the lower (top) to upper (bottom). Consequently, when one encounters an Eintou, one ascends (subconsciously) from Lower to Upper Km.t. on one level of psychospiritual understanding; and one navigates the Dwt on other levels of meaning.

As the year 2000 progressed, I experimented with Eintou musicality. I researched The Blues and realized I could incorporate Blues strategies, beats, and rhythms into the form:

**Urban Blues**
**(a suburbanite's view)**

**Go down**
**in dem streets an'**
**bits o' plantation 'neath ma feets**
**go down in dem streets, bits o' plantation**
**'neath ma feets. Lawd! bits o'**
**slave in eber face**
**I meets**

**in dem**
**streets bits o' slave**
**in eber face I meets. in**
**dem streets eber face I meets be mockin**

**me. Oh  Lawd! down in dem**
**streets eber face be**
**mockin me** [14]

This experimentation  led me to the realization Eintous could be written as standalone expressions, or they could be linked to express larger ideas. To the extent my conception of the Eintou symbolized my children, it seemed a natural conclusion that I should refer to "linked Eintous" not as "stanzas" or "little rooms," but as Mwts or "mothers." As I watched how my children's mother nurtured and taught them, as I observed the love and attention with which She showered them combined with the fact She had the awesome and sole responsibility for protecting and fashioning their ⊔ during gestation, it seemed appropriate linked Eintous should be called Mwts.

I realized and concluded this in May 2000, two weeks before Jabari's 2nd birthday. Excited, I bolted from my office to the living room where She was playing with the children. Until that day, I had not talked with Her about any of my

---

[14] A Blues Eintou incorporating 8-12 bar beat. From Gods, Truth, & Love, Pg 24.

15

research or ideas around the Eintou. I wanted everything to be perfect- or at least completed before I brought it all to Her attention. She had no idea what I was spending so much time and mental resources on. In as much as I was an avid reader and researcher (of various things), She may have just chalked it all up to yet another subject or topic I was trying to understand. Therefore, when I bolted from my office uncharacteristically excited and emotional, I caught Her by surprise. I remember the conversation like it was yesterday:

**I did it! I did it!!**

*You did what?*
**My poetic form, it's done! And...**

*Is that what you've been working on all this time? Poetry!? A poem?*

**No. It's a...**

*Waste of time. No one really reads them. Except for a handful of people, no one cares about poetry. No one's gonna even read the thing. You're excited about nothing. Waste of time.*

And She promptly went back to playing with the children. From that moment on, I never shared with Her any ideas around poetry in general or my Eintou in particular. I almost scrapped the entire "Eintou" idea in that moment.

But I didn't. I kept them between me and the mswt. I would read them Eintous as my son played and my daughter rested in her BJÖRN; I recited them as I lay on the floor in their bedroom between their beds- serenading them to sleep. And I wrote as many as would present themselves to me. But I must admit, and this is a source of regret, it took years for me to publish or share them with the public at large; always looming in the back of my mind- "waste of time."

Eventually, however, people came into my life who encouraged me to share the Eintou. The form went on to be accepted by many poets. From time to time, over the years, I would google the form; it pleased me to no end to see

17

people were writing them. It was not, in final analysis, a "waste of time."

> (I had abandoned the idea of linked Eintous being called Mwts. But I re-instated it after one day listening to a news program that featured a Black woman crying over the recent death of her son at the hands of racist police. They came to symbolize Black mothers' love. I further modified its symbolism when I heard Palestinian Mothers' crying over the bodies of their lifeless children buried beneath homes razed by zionist bombs. When I Gwprwdjt'd Obsidian[15] and listened to mothers world-wide as they cried over children murdered due to racism, religionism, oppression, and other injustices, I could not discern race, ethnicity, or nationality. I could only feel their anguish. I could only sense their resolve to resist.)

This brings me to the book you are currently reading. It is the result of my 14-year-old daughter, Khabira, insisting I write it; insisting this book would bring value to readers; that

---

[15] To Gwprwdjt Obsidian is the process of seeing and understanding things through the collective eyes and experiences of Tp'wy.

many people would want to know the story behind the Eintou's creation; that many people might enjoy reading my early and later Eintous. I am forever deeply indebted to her for that insistence.

And so, dear reader, twenty-four years after I penned the first ever in honor of my son, I present to you the Eintou. I present how and why I developed it; I present, moreover, my hope that it endures within the corpus of poetic forms for as long as people may compose poetry; my hope that wherever or whenever it is encountered, readers and writers understand how it connects Nchi Ya Mababu culture, music, and history to Her diaspora. How it honors Mothers' resolve to resist and triumph over global oppression and injustice; moreover, I hope potential readers and writers understand every Eintou symbolically connects me to and expresses my undying love for my mswt.

May your Eintous be powerful, engaging, and memorable. May your Mwts resist injustice and oppression everywhere.

The obligation of the free is liberation of the oppressed.

26 February 2024

Kfw M Kht
Akintiunde Kofi Camara

# THE EINTOUS OF AKINTIUNDE
(May they engage you where you most desire)

*Illustration 1: Nichi Ya Mababu, Eintou, Gwnhk*

21

1.

## LAST REQUEST

Oh death,
My last true love!
Sing to me one more song
Of my life.  Sing it soft in your
Sweet, slow and tender voice
And take my breath
Away

2.

Eintou
Death's "so?"

Death so
 often speaks to
 us Blacks nowadays that
 no one cares to listen, to hear
 if He has anything
 important to
 impart

# NEW LOVE FALLS

Open
September arms
New love to on me kiss
The colors coolly brought.  Passions
Red my old love never
Said or sought in
Her heat

4.

# STILL AT SEA

Pregnant-
Contracting waves
Waxing,waning- she swells
With ancestral souls in anguished
Labor, to deliver
Centuries of
Stillborn

# SKIES BOUND HOME

Clouds like
Black ships backtrack
Passing midline retrieve
Patrons weighted wet. I wave, "Bon
voyage brothers, sisters
Arrive safely-
Kiss mom."

6.

# BLACK MOON WITHIN ME

She comes
Into my heart, slowly
Settling upon me a darkness that
When complete, reflects my soul: alive in its
Blackness, with her light at its
Core like a night's
Full moon

7.

if you
wonder why we
won't fear the whiteman's hate,
my father said (of us): throw a
cat into the water,
he will not fear
the cold

8.

Dawning Blues

it's worst
 the silence since
 you are gone, oh! baby
 this silence is worst since you're gone
 kinda like that dark thang
 baby before
 the dawn

before
 the dawn baby
 it wants to die.  oh! my
 heart before the dawn wants to die
 baby since you are gone
 Death a' come by
 and by

9.

Oh love,
my soul without
you is as barren as
the infertile womb: presenting
the promise of life's spark
while hopeless of
its fire

10.

death's is

Where I
come from death is
a body, an ocean whose depths
drown king's dream; a thought whose words we
cannot help but speak; a blackness
like asphalt that paves
each street

11.

Lucifer's Lament

At times
my reasoning's so strong
it's impossible to prove me wrong.
It is during these times that (I AM)
most afraid because self righteousness is
the crux of every
god's evil

12.

Lucifer on the Fall
(A plea for Perspicacity)

Every g(o)od
needs a slithering thing
it can fleer and (ex) –scape
its goatish: Judas, Gog and Magog, those used
to conceal its historical diableries; its Hezbollah, its
Al-qaeda and 911 malicious spleens; while
at Abu Ghraibs, w(h)it(e)nesses
go ignored

[16]

---

[16] An early Eintou in which I experimented with eight
lines and two eight syllable/word count Kht's

13.

# Modern Darwinism

(Discover, July 2002, Pp 40-44)

I learned
today: laboratorily separating Rhesus
monkeys from family, and exposing them
to alcohol creates the "alcoholic monkey;" further profiling
and miring them in poverty, drugs,
crime and marginalization creates
the "Nigger"

14.

god's place

In Time's
domain, god's the
transient who loiters
within quarters, the keys to which
Reason (for the moment)
is unable
to find

Drowning

Swimming
in the blood of
our brothers and sisters
we take pride in our back strokes as
whites calculate score cards
like olympic
judges

16.

"...drive them out and destroy them quickly,
just as the Lord has spoken to you." – deut 9:3

(For Hamites, Palestinians, et al)


very at
heart of these genocides
beat abrahams of schizoid polities that
exclaim always our suffering rests within ancient swears
some books of decreed deceit and
imagined Hypocrites who incite
real death

17.

If Death's Then

If Death's
  a whiteman, Fear's
  his city, an inner
  utter immobilizing of
  cracked homes and streets littered
  with our passive
  blackselves

18.

Imagine it

Just like
  shadows and dreams
  we're less is than is is
  cerebral illusion: (we think?)
  consciousness our gods and
  our very selves
  are real

19.

Faded Glory

          a Black
             Dwarf once asked night's
             shade if she remembered
             his name. "yes! It's the Moon's after
             he sets and everyone's
             forced to bloom for
             Sun's rise."

20.

Grammatological Thoughts
For Jacques Derrida

I get
every freakin'
~~idea~~ inkling that
that son-of-a-bitch's unwriting
but what'ssliding through his
understand arche(s)
~~meaning~~

Non-Euclidean Geometry

Circles.
 inside. US. trapped.
 reach for peace, never grasp.
 like china, our walls. yin/yang fragged.
 North Korea bisects.
 think about it.
 dipshits

Control.
 is this the point?
 confines. hyperbolic
 god. satan. parallels. You/me.
 try to move on. and then
 iraq. israel
 circles

22.

blacks emigrate
into the best white
neighborhoods and relinquish their kids' minds
to the best white schools, then are completely
stupefied when they become the best
white citizens society has
to offer

23.

God's Imperatives

(In the beginning was the Word,
and the Word was with God, and the Word was God.)
John 1:1

Without
 (quest)ion my Word's
 more false than biblical
 truth: pure evil exists (within!)
 blind faith and deluded
 religionist
 dogma

You're not
 without Reason
 (fathom!) my solitude's
 pain became the truth of your is:
 living one's self negates
 the whys within
 I'm here

Killer Roaches:
(In Memory of Brother Timothy Thomas)

must had
been quick, how that
roach drew and fired as you
fled.  "They come by tens" Old Lem said-
the other nine must be
hid within the
jury

25.

## On Being and Existence

(Discover, June 2002 Pp. 44-48)
(in memory of John Archibald Wheeler)

Are we
 these physical
 inexactitudes and
 ruminations contained within
 experientially
 delimited
 being

Are we
 merely essence
 therefore interacting
 cognitively within temporal
 manifestation How
 can we really
 exist

Outside
 these boundaries
 what is there that can be
 if I sans your There have no Here
 what needs then noting to(o!)
 make us more than
 these things

46

26.

lust is
a novel-read
hot! the thumbing through which
entertains our passions until
the publishing of love's
monumental
epic

death's dream


When death
sleeps she dreams of
purpled pastures swaying of blue flowers
blossoming into green sky of yellow clouds. she
dreams of life's unimagined all, tearing
with joy, smiling like
a child

28.

don't read
this shakespeare. there is
none of me in here.  rather
read some Baraka or Hughes.  in there is
somethin' i can use. some of
me, an' how to
be free.

29.

# Dancing with Death

Life's slow
 drag and grinding
 apprehension laying
 completely bare our every cant
 prevent from fading to
 night's stillness, day's
 movements

30.

Anonymously
(for everyone)

what their
theys are doin
to them over there our
theys will do to us over here
how do i know? 'cause those
people's every
one watched
others
as every they
did to peoples back then
those same things while all the others
did nothing because they
could not see them
in them

31.

# To Dream

my nights
merrily dance
tunes of sunny whistles
As they smile your blissful breathing
And contemplate how this
Amazing is
too dream

The Tug of War
(A God's Eye Perspective)

Jesus
you're not equipped
for global salvation
your christ was not meant to be more
than a jewish phenom
but you lied stole
copied
others'
belief systems
then claimed to be the way
to world salvation through the years
you have had to crusade
and inquest out
the path

You have(!)
made a complete
mockery of faith now
the islamists are exploding
their version of your lies
ever-ree-where!
you're god(?!)

my God(!?)
Are you insane?
so long as religion
remains general people will
always boykin to bin
laden and vice
versa

33.

## Gods/Religions/man

Encode
upon my mind
contradictions, half-truths
make me recite them in toto
subdue my world such that
B.F. Skinner
would blush

Brainwash
me from my youth
in divine delusions
or corybantic convictions
and I will mow down all
humankind just
because

34.

## Racism's Last Word
### (For Mr. Lott)

Is an
embittered white
proud in his desires for
returns to heinous times: lynchings
burnings, Jim Crow.  He frames
the hate he loves
within

Rightwing
lies spouted in
bursts of incoherent
ribaldry.  Just as he's about
to breathe his last, he smiles,
sobs:  "that Goddamned
Black Man"

35.

## Black Leaders

Once were
 buttocks-kickin,
 agenda-makin, fire
 breathers shot from what some called hell
 locustlikeswarming then
 just stoodstill like
 cackle

In pens
 leftists rightly
 raised to police hapless,
 palsied, abba-dabba Negroes
 with accommodating
 smiles and toothless
 charmings

36.

Christs' Inanities

Combi-
 (nations) of (his)
 torical legacies
 stolen, modified, recycled
 to an unsuspecting
 sleepish masses
 (believe

Me?) I've
 known formulas
 that turn truths into lies
 then into other kinds of truths
 from which genocidal
 lusts and greeds have
 been launched

37.

Thou Will Be Done
(A psuedo-Afrocentric view of Western Heaven)

I will
in heaven be (done)
as I have been on Earth:
Tuskegee'd to the lowest quarters, where cherubs will
syphilize and crack me to madness;
archangels will profile me;
michael's sword

will leave
me wondering whether Earth
was the Eden of Hell; gabriel's
horn will not announce my spirit; and peter's
Pearly Gate greeting will mortify me
to the core: "Sup,
my nigger!"

38.

Portal of Atheism

Beyond naiveté -
above the soul's threshold
faith empties from these shells: body
heart, mind.  Suddenly they make perfect fucking sense-
war, disease, damned debauched holy books.
I know why priests
molest boys,
mothers crack
babies, why it's been-
will always be- this way. What's(?)
always been said is true: shit flows downward,
we are in its path, and
God's in heaven- on
the throne!

39.

Not Mellarmé, Bluesy Jazz

Being
 devoid meaning
 is not that from which we
 spring(?) our of's picayune within
 the world: presence without
 mind belies soul
 we think

 beyond
 syntax there is
 potentiality
 eternal as unrealized
 music was our method
 how we came to
 vanish

 inside
 the rued states; there
 had to be more.  Language(!)
 the soul's insistence on being
 acknowledged.  And writing
 is its crux an-
 sata

Tricksters & God
(organized religion)

Is God
 less imagine than anansi's
 wisdom weaving about man's nature- his
 tend toward (self) indulgence and trickery? Doesn't He
 reveal lies web worlds when myths
 and morals mix with
 man's malice?

Is He (?)
 less real than Earth
 is axial spin as He's spun
 round and round, every nation sewing God into
 its own selfserving will- reducing His
 purest possible Am to
 nationalist sanctimonies

41.

## A Warrior's Ruing

the day
he died, my grandfather
tearfully said, "I had been fightin'
the whiteman for so long, whenever Midnight came
to kiss me, I could not
feel her blackness for
the moon"

## The Poetry of Language

For Charles Bernstein

By this
   time each artificial thing
   and each overtly absorbed fell into
   the universal wastebasket of useless verse; the ink
   from pennings of dead metaphors and
   dangling similes stinking the
   sagacious pages

Of a
   poetics: like animal droppings
   upon forest floors- so much encrusted
   shit.  By this time all that had meaning
   was: formlessness, style and the language
   they tried so vainly
   to contain

# Philosophy

in class
(philosophy)
the professor asked this:
"if a tree in the forest falls
and no one is there to
 hear, does it make
 a sound?"

placing
the thing in his
american heart, I
asked: "if policemen kill a black
man and no one's there to
see it, is he
not dead?"

## Strange Fruit

he sways
peaceful his neck
limp like a baby on
its mother's bosom he stares his
feet longing to reach the
ground so he can
go home

45.

## Outthere

("Then have you arrived at such a degree
of apathy that you take pleasure only in
your disease?  If that is the case, let us fly
to countries that are the likenesses of Death."
Baudelaire)


Out there
 where trees samba
 zephyrs' intimations;
 where coyness is young women, win-
 some on wayward boys' smiles;
 where always this
 brighter

future
lay just beyond
melancholiac now;
where life, as presence, is no feint
and ennui dares not like
some voracious
cara-
cara
gigglegobble
spontaneity; where
Velleity  does not beguile:
"if not out of this mind
perhaps out of
this life"

46.

Future Blues

One day
 we will look back
 at it all, the ways we
 killed one another, the ways we
 destroyed one another;
 we will look back
 and laugh.

One day
 we gon' look back
 at all of it, the lies
 we told ourselves, the religious
 and political ones;
 we gon' look back
 and laugh

At all
 we tawt we was,
 de individuel-
 isms, ists; we gon' look back an'
 laff 'way blacks done wen dey
 list' to an' sung
 dey blues

47.

For the Truth Initiate
(upon earning heirs mark)

Seeker
 (explore all paths!)
 through godly leaning selves
 as illusions they're central to(o!)
 reality's labyrinths
 tread slowly thus
 by ways
 (of facts:)
 pursue without
 motive malice or will
 when thus freed (your mind of hearts) to
 untwine cosmic strings, you'll
 unravel t(His
 secret):

The Truth
 does not exist
 in gods or sciences;
 it's not in you, seeker, others
 nor things sought, but withal(l)
 standingunder
 our real

48.

Keeping it Real
(From God with contempt)

I can't...
 please understand,
 relaying this makes it
 hard to hold back the laughter from
 you who are so little
 but want so much
of me

...Your faiths?
(emptinesses
 drawn from your own psyches,
 from your need to believe in you)
 have nothing to do with
 my divine Plan(?)
You?  My

image?
(with your "Holy"
Wars, your disease, with your
deceits-why you sons of bitches
even murder, molest
and abandon
your own

children!)
you're pathetic...
you were never more than
amusements or distractions- play
things I created to
relieve weekend
ennui

49.

Theophany
(A Poem Reveals its is)

without
i am context
within social milieux
which is the source of all debate
banal/academic
philosophic
ethnic

read me (?)
Macleish said it
(best too): just let me be!
but in being i must become
specially when (marr)|(ed)
(by your thinking)
to thought

I won't
ever just be
text without con (for you)
i will always be a means to-
ward some sort of social
historical
self end

at this
precise moment
(ten to the minus four
tee third second) I have become
your wasams and (will)
shape your future
ises

within
this I ever shift(s)
identity purpose
and being about your being
in this sense i am THAT
I AM and thus
your god

74

50.

@ the Foot of god's Sarcophagus
(For Joseph Campbell)

Jesus
don't you under
stand(?) you were not my first
manGod!  The truth is fossilized
in my primitive brain
only to be
unearthed

as I
Campbell through myths
superstitions and our
desires to make sense of the world
and cosmic mysteries
it's my natures
(I must

grasp): you
 represent a
 more recent matrix of
 psuedo-rationales intended
 to breathe order into
 incongruent
 being

 You've failed
 for these (Reasons)
 I inter you within
 this sarcophagus: Jesus Christ(!)
 watch science lime your flesh
 that I may free
 my soul

51.

## Paralogism
(after Heidegger)

My life
 this historic
 Dasein of unknown force.
 I rise above my mind within
 this now (whose being moves
 outside my grasp)
 into
 a past
 whose blast shapes all
 of my dark matterings;
 I marvel at its nebulous
 beauty, cower before
 the awe of its
 vastness.

At once
 captivated
 by and fearful of its
 paradoxically confined
 openness, I long to
 devour it with
 my thought,
 knowing
 in some foreign
 region of my being
 in time merely present-at-hand,
 I'll never bound beyond
 this poetic
 dwelling

ANATOMY OF THE EINTOU

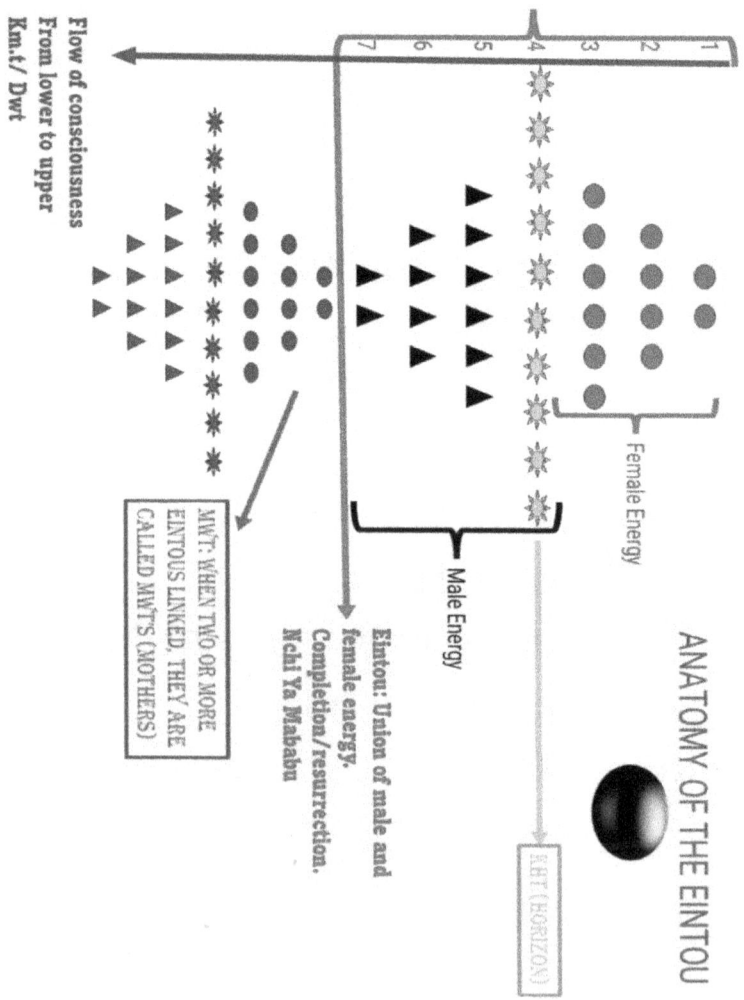

Flow of consciousness
From lower to upper
Km.t / Dwt

MWT: WHEN TWO OR MORE
EINTOUS LINKED, THEY ARE
CALLED MWT'S (MOTHERS)

Eintou: Union of male and
female energy.
Completion/resurrection.
Nehi Ya Mababu

Male Energy

Female Energy

ANATOMY OF THE EINTOU

EHT (HORIZON)

# COMPILATIONS

Front Cover Illustrations

1.) An Eintou (Black Pearl) superimposed with Mdw Ntr Yry N ("born of"). This is laid over Lower Nchi Ya Mababu (Land of the Ancestors) to symbolize the Eintou is Born of that continent.

2.) Within Nchi Ya Mababu's silhouette, are the various instruments used to perform blues and jazz.

3.) Two rows of Tp'w extending back to p't nnw p't (beginnings of beginnings)

4.) DunDun ('talking drum"). Primary means through which I communicate with Tp'w during ceremonies.

Back Cover Illustrations

1.) Nchi Ya Mababu (Land of the Ancestors

2.) Basso: musical symbol used in jazz and blues notation.

3.) Dundun: "Talking Drum"

4.) Musical notes and symbols (in the background)

5.) Gwnhk symbol (above rearing horse): symbolizes cyclic, energetic infinity and the connections binding us to Tp'w.
6.) Rearing horse draped with broken chains symbolizes my family breaking the chains of enslavement and rising from the Ma'afa.
7.) The rearing horse stands on an open book, symbolizing knowledge is how we keep the chains of bondage from entangling us.

Body Illustrations

## Terms & Phrases

## References

Asante, Molefi Dr. (1991). The Book of African Names. Africa World Press

Kht, Kfw (2024). Gods, Truth, & Love. Illinois. Akintiunde Press

Gardiner, Alan Sir (2020). Egyptian Grammar: Third Edition, Revised. United Kingdom. Peeters Publishers-Leuven

Giroux, Joan (1999). The Haiku Form. United States. Barnes & Noble, Inc.

McCarthy, Josephine (2022). The Book of Gates. United Kingdom. TaDehent Books

Petty, Bill PhD.(2016) English To Middle Egyptian Dictionary. Colorado. Museum Tours Press

## Contact Kfw

Phone: 414-807-6534

Facebook: Kfw M Kht

You Tube: Kfw Kht

X (Formerly Twitter): Kf.w M Kht

Email: Balantamd3@aol.com


## Other Works by Kfw M Kht
(Available on Amazon)

Gods, Truth, & Love

Awakenings: Entrances Into Consciousness, Reality, and Being

Awakenings II: Everything Is Symbol